Sister
God Bless You!

Love's Survivor

Eph 3:20
God give you more than you ask...!

Charlotte Johnet
Love you in Jesus

Love's Survivor

My Testimony of How I Survived The Greatest Love Story Ever Told

Charlotte Jolivet

AuthorHouse™
1663 Liberty Drive
Bloomington, IN 47403
www.authorhouse.com
Phone: 1-800-839-8640

© *2012 by Charlotte Jolivet. All rights reserved.*

No part of this book may be reproduced, stored in a retrieval system, or transmitted by any means without the written permission of the author.

First published by AuthorHouse   02/10/2012

ISBN: 978-1-4670-6088-2 (sc)
ISBN: 978-1-4670-6087-5 (hc)
ISBN: 978-1-4670-6086-8 (ebk)

Library of Congress Control Number: 2011918191

Printed in the United States of America

Any people depicted in stock imagery provided by Thinkstock are models, and such images are being used for illustrative purposes only.
Certain stock imagery © *Thinkstock.*

This book is printed on acid-free paper.

Because of the dynamic nature of the Internet, any web addresses or links contained in this book may have changed since publication and may no longer be valid. The views expressed in this work are solely those of the author and do not necessarily reflect the views of the publisher, and the publisher hereby disclaims any responsibility for them.

Contents

Introduction vii

Chapter One—A Marriage Gone Bad 1

Chapter Two—A Time of Prosperity 17

Chapter Three—Spiritual Oppression 23

Chapter Four—Reflections 33

Chapter Five—"I'll Never Go Back" 41

Chapter Six—Help! What . . . ??? 53

Chapter Seven—Breaking Point to Victory 69

Acknowledgement 93

Prayer of Salvation 95

My Memorial Stones Pictures 107

Introduction

God created us with great purpose, potential, and capacity to be filled with the fullness of God. There is nothing in life that does not display His handiwork. Our purpose as human beings, created by Him, is to display His love for us. Think about it, if you have children of your own you want only the best for them. When you give them your best and they wear it well, it brings glory to you. People around you say, "Wow, that man (or woman) really knows how to take good care of their children!" When we subdue by resisting the enemy we are telling the world that God is all powerful and that we, as His children, can do all things through Him and are well taken care of. We tell the story of His power and riches, His love, and His purpose as we yield to His instructions through His written Word, the Bible, or through His revealed Word by our relationship with Him. Yes, God still speaks to His children today. This relationship between God and his children is the greatest love story every told. The symbiotic connection of the love of a true father for his children as seen through God's plan of redemption is the greatest example of this extraordinary love, where he makes all things new.

We are love letters from God, His epistles to be read by all men. According to the bible in 2 Corinthians 3:2-6:

"Ye are our epistle written in our hearts, known and read of all men: Forasmuch as ye are manifestly declared to be the epistle of Christ ministered by us, written not with ink, but with the Spirit of the living God; not in tables of stone, but in fleshly tables of the heart. And such trust

have we through Christ to God-ward: Not that we are sufficient of ourselves to think anything as of ourselves; but our sufficiency is of God; Who also hath made us able ministers of the new testament; not of the letter (law), but of the spirit: for the letter killeth, but the spirit giveth life."

In the movie industry today, we see Hollywood producers who entertain us with their interpretations of life and death, good and evil, or love and hate. They are no match for the glory of God. He set things in motion at the cross and defeated evil, and set us free to experience the power of His goodness and love. I stepped into a real world of living colors and each step was like a 3D screen, where I learned the art of love. There, the Divine Artist started creating in me a heart that looks like my heavenly Father's heart. My hope is for you to go deeper into the secrets of God's love.

He has tattooed you in the palm of his hands for your good and His greater glory. To God be the glory and honor. *Thanks be to God who always causes us to triumph.* We win!

We must realize that we have an enemy who still seeks to kill, steal, and destroy (John 10:10). Jesus gained a great victory over Satan, death, hell, and the grave at the cross. However, the influences of Satan were not removed from the earth. Satan was given legal rights, when Adam disobeyed in the garden. The Bible says he is the god of **this** world. There is a warfare that those who remain must subdue. We are to demonstrate this great victory throughout our Christian walk, understanding that *we are more than conquerors through Him that loved us!* (Roman 8:37).

When we obey the Word of God, we win! We are His victory demonstrated, remembering that *the weapons of our warfare are not carnal, but they are mighty through*

God to the pulling down of strong holds . . . . (2Corinthians 10:4). This is our victory; this is how we win!

Inside the human spirit where is the will to win. 1 Corinthians 13:8 tells us, *"Love never fails,"* This means that love conquerors all. Love is universal because God is love. I hope that as you read about the awesomeness of God's love and protection in this story, your life will be forever changed. My testimony is the story of how God loved me and my family through a period of many dangers. I promised God I would tell it to His glory. I pray that you receive healing and greater insight into God's heart, and greater insight into our fallen nature which will move us into greater intimacy.

I know you will be blessed, encouraged, your faith will come alive, and built up in the love of God. You will find purpose and destiny when seeking greater intimacy with Jesus. There is no need to fail in any area of your life whether it's your health, marriage, relationships, business, or school. Once we understand the art of love and the power of God we succeed.

Chapter One
A Marriage Gone Bad

"Zacchaeus was a wee little man and a wee little man was he...." my baby son, Kenyatta, began to sing as we drove home from Lakewood Church one night. His older brother and sister joined in and we sang all the way to Spaulding Street.

"Momma, my teacher said Jesus is coming to my house," Kenyatta announced as we came to a stop in our driveway.

"That's right, baby, just like the Bible says," I replied with a nod.

The kids piled out of the car. As I walked to the front door, a strange feeling came over me; something had come to our home. Whatever it was made my hand shake as I turned the key in the lock. Inside, my house was not my home anymore, everything was gone . . . all gone! Not one of us breathed or moved. The sudden boom of a voice from somewhere made my children draw close around me in the empty living room.

"KNEFIDIYAMATO!" "KNEFIDIYAMATO!"

I ran to the back door to look out. In less than the two hours we'd spent at church, something evil had taken all of the furnishings in our home—the dressers, the tables, the refrigerator, the stove, all our clothes—and had thrown them into our backyard.

I grabbed my children closer. We dropped to our knees and began to pray. What was I praying? Everything! "Help, God! Oh, God!" I closed my eyes for a moment, when the cold metal of a gun barrel touched the side of my face. Pretending to keep my eyes tightly shut, they were open just enough for me to make out a man's hands and legs.

I knew him!

Oh my God!

It was Ralph, my husband!

"KNEFIDIYAMATO!"

He opened his mouth, but instead of English that crazy chant came out again and again. Those crazy sounds he made seemed to pump him full of strength. He even seemed taller as I dared to look at him past the gun barrel.

The children were now all crying, trying to pray and struggling to say the word, "Daddy."

"We're taking daddy to hheeelllll," a witchy high pitched voice replied.

Next, the voice changed to a voice I knew so well, but this time this familiar voice was one which held hatred and anger that could only have come from hell. My husband said, "If you don't get out of this house now, I'll kill all of you, chop you up, and put the pieces in the fridge in the backyard."

The next voice I heard had no panic in it at all, but peace and love. It was the still, small voice deep within me saying, "The devil wants to kill the entire family."

The Lord had never told me to leave before, but then He said, "Get up off your knees and go!"

I jumped up, grabbed my children and ran.

* * *

In February of 1949, I came into this world to my parents, who at that time resided in Lake Charles, Louisiana. As a baby I had no perception of life. I did not know if the economy was up or down, what war was being fought, or what the weather was that day or who was President. They taught me all they could in order that I would grow and succeed in life. As a child I was taught that the Ten

Commandments contained God's only commandment with promise: *"Children obey your parents that your days may be long and it will go well with you."* I obeyed them in some things, but in others I wanted my own way. I made choices trying to fit in. However, my will was quickly being shaped by my surroundings. They sent me to school, fed, clothed me, provided shelter, and gave me their love trying to train me according to the Word.

We came to Texas when I was one, and lived in Beaumont. We lived there for one year, and the following year we relocated to Houston and lived in an area commonly known as First Ward. I lived with my parents, Charlie and Ollie Ross, and my three sisters. It was considered the poorest part of Houston, and we were considered the poorest of the poor.

There, in First Ward, prostitution, drugs, alcoholism, homelessness, and crime in general were the way of life. It was all around me, but praise be to God, my mother was a Christian! She regularly attended church and taught Sunday school. My mom's godliness was our protection. She made us feel safe and secure in spite of our dad never being home.

My dad loved to drink whiskey, and he drank a lot of it. He worked as a chef in some of Houston's finest restaurants; this was reminiscent of when he met my mom in Louisiana, where they were both chefs. He would go to work early in the morning, and sometimes we would not see him until the next day. He might have had a drinking problem, but he never missed a day of work. When he did come home, we are all happy to see him. He was never abusive and we loved him. At the time I did not know he was a functional alcoholic.

We moved many times, and one day my parents moved my siblings and I—Nancy, Queenie, Mamie, Elizabeth, Betty, Charlie, Ollie, Robert, Fred, Lorenzo, and Alverta—(as you can see our family had grown quite a bit), to Trinity Gardens, which I thought was a better area, of Houston, Texas. As teens our lives began to develop and mature. At the age of eleven years old I gave my life to Jesus at Pleasant Hill Missionary Baptist Church, due in part to my mother's influence most of my siblings received Christ at an early age. The majority of us finished high school, graduating from Kashmere High.

I met my husband, Ralph, through my older sister Nancy. She attended classes with him at Kashmere High. One night on a long, dark road, where I'd followed my two sisters Nancy and Queenie, on a joy ride with their boyfriends, Ralph and I met. I was about thirteen, and thought Ralph loved me very much. He gave me gifts and plenty of money. I must say to the children of today, you must not confuse sex with love, as I later came to realize. True love has nothing to do with sex, gifts, and money; they are two totally different things. True love comes from God (the word is agape in the Greek), it's unconditional and self giving and we must have His love in all relationships. There are three other Greek words for love. We have friendship love; *phileō,* parent love; storgē, and sexual love; eros. Each of these human types of love will fail if not founded on agape, God's love.

Let Jesus teach you the true art of Love. Jesus is our greatest example of true love. Any time we sin we break the heart of God. I hurt both my parents and God when I sinned by committing fornication with Ralph. Mom had always confessed as for me and my house we will serve the Lord.

One night when mom arrived home from work she opened her bedroom door and to her surprise Ralph and I had fallen asleep in her bed. Mom beat us the whole time she was preaching to us, a house divided will not stand, she preached. The shame and guilt I felt that night was overwhelming, but I could not break through the stronghold of lust. Sin will take you further than you want to go because you go against God's love for you. When practicing sin you are leaving his protection and breaking fellowship. When we repent we restore our fellowship with God who always loves us. Sin hurts the Fathers heart but He forgives us. When living in sin we do not love ourselves the way God does, when he says, "love yourself as you do others". You must be born again of the Spirit and accept and acknowledge God's love because true love comes from Him. Those who love God will keep His commandments.

I did not love myself. My nickname was Fatso and I saw myself that way; fat and ugly. I did not see myself as God saw me. We need to see ourselves as God sees us: His creation. In Genesis, after He created all things, after He made us in his own image and likeness, after he breathed life into us and we became a living soul, He looked and said, *"It is very good"*. He was well pleased and loved his creation in its purity. It was not until Adam and Eve ate from the tree of knowledge of good and evil that they discovered their nakedness, their fallen nature, and they saw themselves unclean, yet God still loved them. His love is pure and undiluted by man's sinful nature.

He only wants what is best for us. That is why it is my prayer that every person will remain pure until marriage. Marriage is a picture of Christ and the church, for Christ sees the church as His bride, holy and beautiful.

Later, in a backslidden condition and one month pregnant, I became engaged to Ralph. We married when I was fifteen and he was nineteen. Ralph was four years older than me to the day. Isn't it phenomenal that we would have the same birthday, February 10, during the love month. I had no thought for whether he was born again or not, all I knew was that I was in love and on cloud nine and that Ralph was my "knight in shining armor". I thought of abortion, but there was a struggle deep down within me that knew from my up bringing abortion was murder. I believed marriage was the right thing to do because my sisters by this time were married to the love of their lives. I had no idea what true love was anyway. I had no true frame of reference because I did not understand God's love for me. I lived in a dream world. It was as though I was living and playing inside of a doll house during my first year of marriage.

I dropped out of school in the ninth grade to give birth to our first child, Elaine. Ralph was a good man by the world's standard. He was considerate of my needs, hard working, a wonderful husband, and a wonderful father. His parents, Ezekiel and Beatrice moved to Houston with their family of sixteen children from Baldwin, Louisiana in 1956. Ralph thought it was one of the darkest days of his life! He felt he was leaving the stillness and beauty of the country life he loved so well. There he'd even swim sometimes in the bayous with the alligators.

He often boasts that his father taught him the importance of hard work and learning a skill. All of us called Ezekiel, "Pop". His favorite saying was "exercise your muscle or exercise your brain", meaning don't be idle—get a job or go to school. All his children knew this requirement, and as a result many of Ralph's siblings are very successful. They had a strong work ethic and were very intelligent. They were allowed to choose to go to church. In contrast, my mother dragged us to church every time the doors were open. She was also very strict when it came to moral living. In his later years, Ralph's father had a supernatural experience with God and was called to preach the gospel.

Everyone could see that Ralph and I were made for each other. We were a new kind of Romeo and Juliet. Our love was beautiful, and our marriage was one made in heaven, or so I thought. My opinion of marriage at that time, however, came from what I saw on television. My parents had challenges because of my father's drinking. I did have an aunt and uncle from Louisiana, Uncle Charlie and Aunt Ethel, who had a marriage that was peaceful and full of love. They were both Christians and teachers of The Word, but at the time I never made the connection that living a godly, Christian lifestyle could have this impact on a marriage. I was content to stay out of school and simply care for our daughter, Elaine. Ralph encouraged me to return to high school. I did, and graduated in 1968. Everyone, me included, was very proud that I completed my high school education even though I did not like school or studying, and did just enough to pass. All I wanted was to be a wife and mother. I was glad when graduation day came, now I was able to focus on my family.

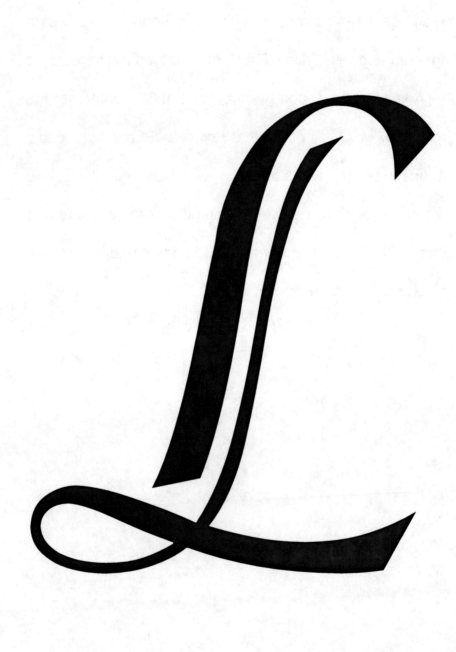

Chapter Two

A Time of Prosperity

𝓕ast forwarding five years, I began to pray for a male child. He would be a gift from God to the man I loved very much. My husband's gift arrived July 11, 1970. He was joyfully named Ralph Jolivet, Jr., our second child, better known as "Skid Row", a nickname given him by his dad. We were happy and our home was a happy one. Interestingly, in a city "Skid Row" is known as an area of cheap bars and run down hotels, frequented by alcoholics and vagrants. Be careful how you give your children nicknames. Your confession brings possession (Proverbs 18:21).

Ralph had a vision to become self-employed. This vision was fulfilled when he opened an automotive shop on Spaulding Street not far from where we lived. Later we were able to buy our first home. I was a stay-at-home mom to our two children, never having to work. I get joy when I think back to those days and about the goodness of God. I was intrigued with my new life. I would often catch myself singing my favorite song, "I am the Happiest Girl in the whole USA." That's how I truly felt. Everything was going so well! Unfortunately, this did not continue. I was surprised and hurt when the turnaround happened. I was a Christian who did not understand the love of God, our fallen nature, or spiritual warfare, and I was soon to discover them all.

Ralph's Automotive Mechanic Shop became a place where many of his friends began to hang out. I'll never forget when Ralph told me his friends called him "henpecked." It hurt him deeply for he was never henpecked. He was just a man who loved his family and took care of us, unlike some of the others who were cheating on their wives, drinking, and getting into all kinds of trouble. At that time, Ralph did none of those things, then one day he told me, "I'm going to go down to come back up better". I begged him not to change and told him that I loved him the way he was.

A short while later my mother called to ask if I'd drive her someplace. When she came out of the house she had on her special holy missions' hat, and her "big gun" Bible under her arm. Her lips were moving in serious prayer.

As a girl I had often gone door-to-door with my mother witnessing and praying for the sick. It was not unusual for God to have awakened her with a burning desire to go and visit some family in need. This was very puzzling to me because I felt we were the ones in need. I figured this was such a case. She gave me one of her church offering envelopes with an address scribbled across the top.

I spoke in surprise, "That's my address. That's Ralph's shop, Momma!"

When we arrived at the shop, Ralph was bending over a car checking something under the hood. We drove up and I blew the horn. He looked up. His grin as he saw my mother grew bigger and bigger. He ran over to us and said, "Como-ca vi, Cherie Madam".

Ralph's love for my mother was expressed in Creole French. There were kisses all around. He pulled up a few chairs, seating us in a cool spot, just to the side of his office. We sat far enough away that we could not hear a bunch of his buddies commenting, laughing, and giving each other high fives. With one hand on her Bible and the other on her son-in-law's knee, my mother started by saying, "Son, don't you know that 'down' is the devil?"

"Madam, I'm going down to come up better! I'm going to be bigger. It's like I told Charlotte, I'm coming up right. Oh, yes I am!" Ralph almost yelled.

My mother answered him, "'Down' is the devil, son. 'Up' is God."

A customer drove up; Ralph got up to take care of him. As I watched him walk away from us, I wanted to put my head in my mother's lap and cry. I knew Ralph thought his way was right, but when we make choices from mere human reasoning we can't see the big picture ahead. Leaning to your own understanding can lead to all sorts of trouble. Only God knows the future. Let Him lead you into the path that is right, not just seems right. The Word says, *"There is a way that seems right to a man, but its end is the way of death."* (Proverbs 14:12 NKJV

Chapter Three

Spiritual Oppression

During this time I did not realize it, but I too was experiencing an outrageous demonic attack. The devil is a liar. He was a liar from the beginning when he deceived Eve and convinced Adam to disobey God's perfect plan for mankind. He was a liar when he told Adam and Eve they were going to be as God. By listening to these lies they lost their connection with the true and living God who made them. Adam and Eve took on the nature of the devil who is the god of this world where sin, pain and toil was introduced. If you believe the lie of the devil, you become that lie. He is a liar still today when he convinces God's children to stray from the path chosen for them. *"The devil is a liar and the father of lies"*, John 8:44.

Now I know this, but I didn't know it then. I remember the moment the demons attacked my mind. It was a beautiful night, believe it or not, the skies were clear but my thoughts were cloudy. The devil bombarded my mind with thoughts that Ralph was falling out of love with me. In my anger, I murmured, "Bad God!" When I said those words, it was as if I felt a great weight drop on my back and an awful fear came upon me. The demons told me, "You have blasphemed and will never go to heaven." This frightened me immensely! I had just begun seeking the Lord through His Word, desiring to know this God who had given me such a beautiful loving husband and family. I, Charlotte Jolivet, love my husband, Ralph Jolivet, for better or for worse, for richer or poorer, in sickness and in health, until death do us part. I love him still and those are vows I was determined to keep. This was a covenant we made not only with ourselves but with God. Scripture says, "Let the weak say I'm strong and let the poor say I'm rich." When we declare God's Word then we are able to call situations that have gotten worse better and the poor areas of our lives richer. When death prevails it's only temporary because those of us who are saved have received eternal life. A desire deep within me to draw closer to God, who is the author and sustainer of our love; I was only barely beginning to understand the love of God and I did not want to fail Him. Yet the fear increased. Still I went into a great depression.

All the while I kept pursuing God, praying, reading my Bible. I came across verses I knew were the truth, and the truth you know is the truth that will make you free! I knew, *". . . no weapon formed against me would prosper."* (Isaiah 54:11) I also knew, *". . . nothing could separate me from the love of God."* (Romans 8:35) That means no principalities, no powers, and no rulers. If I would continue to seek Him first with all my heart I would find Him. *". . . and ye shall seek me, and find me, when ye shall search for me with all your heart. And I will be found by you, saith the LORD: and I will turn away your captivity . . ."* (Jeremiah 29:13, 14) We are powerful!

Our Father has not left us without authority. We have His Word, the power of prayer, the Holy Spirit, and angels that are fighting on our behalf to survive. The Word of God says, *"He that cometh to me, I will in no wise cast out."* (John 6:37 KJV) I was determined to keep pressing into the things of God. Even though I was at an extremely low point I knew that God could deliver me and that every promise he made in the bible was for me, too.

When all dreams and hope are lost you are not to give in because you are going to make it. Hope deferred makes the heart sick, but when desires comes it is a tree of life (Proverbs 13:12). I can declare that the enemy cannot stop you from the tree of life, when you keep the faith. I must stop here and say: oppression, depression, worry, and even stress are all tricks of the enemy! The devil almost got me off God's plan for my life. He wants to stop you, and me, from seeking God. Listen, my brother, my sister, if you feel that you have blasphemed God, repent of those negative thoughts and actions, believe that God is faithful to forgive, and keep seeking Him. Be assured, you have not blasphemed if your heart is to keep seeking and obeying God.

Don't run *from* God, run *to* God. Stop chasing the dream and chase the dream giver. Don't let your dream become an idol that separates you from God. It's never too late to dream again. Dream big!

The demons attempted to stop me from giving myself totally to God, but their best efforts were not good enough. God wants all of me, not a part time lover. As I was going to a revival meeting, at the little family church I attended at that time, intent upon pressing into the things of God, the demons jumped on my back and knocked me to my knees. Literally, jumped on my back and knocked me to my knees. I got up and staggered, pushing against the force of evil that was pulling me back. With intense effort, I planted one foot onto the church grounds. Still, a force threw me back, pulled me away from the entrance, and away from the church building, away from God's teachings that would be my hope of help. I tried to get into the building; I knew if I could just get in, I would hear the gospel and its power would be able to deliver me. So, steadfast, burdened, weighted, I staggered trying to get up to the church door. When I entered, the preacher was beginning his message, and my ears suddenly stopped up. This was some serious spiritual warfare. Evil forces were fighting to try and keep me from truly knowing God. Religion will allow you to know about God, but it lacks the intimacy needed to know Him. He did not die for religion, He wanted a family relationship. The depression deepened and I could not stop crying. I felt my husband didn't love me anymore, and even felt I was a bad mother to our children. This added to my pain, I was teaching them the Word but when it came to the sports at school, I would send then on their way and rarely showed up at any of their games.

I lost all desire to go anywhere besides church. At this time Ralph took me to the doctor (thank God for doctors) to fight the depression, but I soon realized that this was a waste of time; a spiritual battle cannot be fought in the natural realm. I cried for a whole year, so hurt and so wounded because I was listening to the voice of the enemy. Nothing was getting any better because I was not listening to the voice of a loving and a good God, my Heavenly Father. When the devil did that to me, I almost got stuck. My life was as if I was in a "maze," each turn was a dead end. I experienced such pain and suffering, and I began to try and figure out life. But praise God, He wasn't going to allow the devil to steal my future. God always want us to press forward, for our latter is greater than our beginning. Never get stuck! Just keep believing in His promises. He wants the greater good for our life.

My aunt Bessie convinced my mother to take me to see a Pentecostal bishop and family friend from the church she attended. After he, with the church elders, cast demons out of me, he went on to explain the spiritual battle I was fighting. He told me how the battle was in the mind, and instructed me to put the Word of God inside me, in my heart and my mind, and to pull up any bad thoughts that entered in. This, he explained, was how I would be delivered. He described how my mind was like a garden, and if I plant good things in my garden then good would grow. However, if I allowed bad things into my garden, things I did not desire to grow, I needed to pull those things up like unwanted weeds. He went on to say that I needed *to be renewed in the spirit of my mind* (Ephesians 4:23). I did this diligently and was completely delivered from depression and mental torment. Out of my deliverance, my love for the Lord grew stronger and I began to hunger and thirst for more of God. I wanted to know Him more and more and the power of His resurrection.

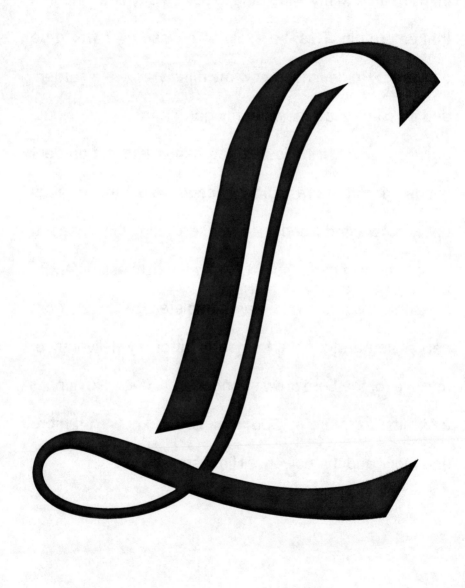

Chapter Four
Reflections

How we tend to fall in love seems so strange. How we look at one another with starry eyes in the beginning? He opens doors for you and we try so hard to please each other, that we don't see the red flags, but when the love is not so new anymore it can begin to sour. This is what happened to our marriage. Ralph stopped doing all the little things he'd done when we were first married. I'm sure I did also. Our honeymoon stage was slowly coming to an end. Oh, he was still kind to me in a way. He would let me cry on his shoulders like before, but I could tell the difference. In the beginning Ralph drank socially but then his drinking increased. He seemed to be trying to please his friends more than his wife and family. He wanted to show them he was not "henpecked!" All along I was begging, "Please, I love you. Don't go down that road." At this time my favorite song was, *The Way We Were,* by Barbara Streisand. It always reminded me of the beautiful, intelligent, sensitive, talented, caring man my husband once was.

In the beginning Ralph drank whenever he wanted since he owned the shop and there was no boss or supervisor to answer to. Later, 'whenever he wanted' became all the time. Ralph used to say, "'he never met a stranger,'" everyone was his friend, Miles, Massad and Luchin as well as others, were always encouraging him to do well. Murphy, a friend of Ralph's, also known as 'the dog man,' was always hanging around the shop. Murphy loved his dogs he trained them to do unbelievable tricks. I believed, the dogs were Murphy's idols, just as drinking and working had become Ralph's idols. Idols are not merely carved images in Africa, or some other foreign country where the people have not been introduced to our Lord and Saviour Jesus Christ. God showed me an idol is anything you put before Him. Here in America we have all sorts of idols car rims, homes, money, celebrities, anything can become an idol. The Lord says, *"You shall have no other gods before Me."* (Exodus 20:3 NKJV)

Ralph and I continued this way for many years as the years passed the drinking soon overpowered Ralph. He began to run from the law due to traffic tickets for driving under the influence. He would fight with the police right on our front lawn. One day Ralph had a huge altercation with the police when they came to arrest him, a SWAT (Special Weapons and Tactics) team was called to the scene—the 'scene' being right in front of our home. Ralph hid behind the house while drawing his gun; the SWAT team then drew their weapons in all readiness to fire. It was only a speeding ticket, but when Ralph drank, a new kind of crazy rebellion possessed him. Alcohol had truly become a serious and deadly problem for him, hurting people hurt others.

Our marriage was going down the drain. I began praying for a job, asking the Lord to help me find employment so I could help take care of our children. Although I had attended business training school I'd never worked, and unfortunately I was unable to find a job. Ralph's behavior changed drastically. He stopped going to church and even burned money on the stove while cursing us. He did, however, manage to pay the mortgage off as he ran his auto shop out of our garage. Ralph gave from his heart. He had given some of his friend's deals on their auto repairs, and these arrangements with buddies left little money to bring home to the family. He didn't seem to value his skills or his talent. I needed a job, and bad. God did ultimately give me one—supernaturally, where I retired after thirty years from the U.S. Post Office, but that's another miracle story. I left the children at home and went to work, but Ralph didn't like me making my own money or working long hours. The communication became nonexistence.

Ralph's drinking continued to become more and more outrageous. He drank day and night. His favorite drink was MD2020, also known as 'mad dog' 2020. I was sick and tired of our lifestyle. We worked and he drank, fussed, and was destroying the life we'd been building for years. I reached a breaking point and could not take it anymore, so I left and took the children with me, but he came and got us, promising us all he would do better. Nevertheless, nothing was working. I was by this time a miserable, hurt woman and wanted out, I wanted a divorce. It felt like I was losing my best friend, my love—the love of my life—and my life. It was like I was sleeping with the enemy. I prayed, "God, what do you want me to do?" He led me to 1 Corinthians 7:14 tell us, *"For the unbelieving husband is sanctified by the wife, and the unbelieving wife is sanctified by the husband."* I said, "I know I am sanctified. Therefore, according to Your Word, Lord, You will sanctify my husband." Jesus backed up His word and said to me, audibly, "I will save your husband."

There were two things I had to do. One, I had to stay pure. Two, I had to tell this testimony all over the world. I said, "Yes," to both and promised God I would, which seemed impossible to do, at the time. When I said, I would, the Divine Artist colored this as love. I left my mother's house and we went back home to try and make things good, but things only got worse. Ralph would pull me as I was sleeping out of bed in the middle of the night, put a gun to my head, curse me and make all kinds of threats. I would curse him back until it was shown to me in the Word that cursing and blessing should not come from the same mouth. From the outside looking in one would say that my life was seriously one big mess, but I was becoming a worshipping warrior. His praises shall continually be in my mouth.

I started choosing to make right choices on purpose, and trusting in His Word—Proverbs 3:5-6 (NKJV)—*"Trust in the LORD with all your heart, and lean not on your own understanding; in all your ways acknowledge Him, and he shall direct your path."*

Chapter Five

"I'll Never Go Back"

I was attending the Baptist Church and had a surprising encounter with God. It was there I received the baptism in the Holy Ghost, with the evidence of speaking in tongues (Acts 2:4). Nobody laid hands on me. It was our choir's annual day and I had been seeking more of God. During the service, I was in the choir praising the Lord, when I had a vision of Jesus bleeding and suffering on the cross for our sins. Such love washed over me for my Saviour that I could not express it in English, and the words just came bubbling up out of me. The church members came running to me after church asking what I was saying, and what had happened to me. I went to my pastor and told him about the experience. He said me that he heard me speaking in tongues, that he knew it was in the Bible, but he did not teach it. He had such love for God that he told me I could speak in tongues anytime I wanted to. Although he did not prohibit me, the Baptists were unable to help me grow in this area as they did not teach on the gifts of the Holy Spirit with the manifestation of speaking in other tongues (1 Corinthians 12:10).

Even though the leaders did not know much about speaking in tongues, they didn't kick me out of the church which I appreciated. My foundation was from this Baptist Church, I still have many lifelong friends at that church. God, bless the Baptists! Since I did not know of a church where the gifts of the Holy Spirit were taught with the manifestation of speaking in tongues, I asked my sister if she did. I desired to know more about this wonderful encounter with the precious Holy Spirit, and she directed me to Lakewood Church. I made my first visit to Lakewood. Praise God! What the devil meant for evil at my former church with all the painful experiences, persecutions, and misleadings, God turned it around for my good. With this new dimension of the Holy Spirit, a greater understanding of God's Word and love was opened to me. This experience changed me forever. Without the power of the Holy Spirit upon me I would not have had the strength to endure the struggle ahead. I hope every believer would receive this power the Baptism of the Holy Spirit. Ask and believe and you will receive.

The night Ralph held a gun to our heads; I'd left my home vowing that I would never go back. Never say 'never', because God is faithful and He always has the last word. Although the Spirit led me to leave that night, He also told me to never let my love for Ralph die from my heart. God gave me His agape love for Ralph. Agape love is an awesome unconditional love of God! It is the fruit of the Holy Spirit. That's why this is one of the greatest love stories ever told! This love should be seen in the heart of His people. The bible says we shall know them by their love. It's a story not about wine and roses or of stolen passion (lust), but a true story about the love of God for His children. Love (God's agape), never fails (1Corinthians 13:8). In the natural the whole world will watch the romance of a man and woman like Diana Princess of Wales, and Charles, Prince of Wales now there son William and Kate.

My Heavenly Father wants to show his supernatural love and goodness to all generations. Isn't it amazing that God loved Ralph through me? His eternal plan is that each one reaches one. Regardless of Ralph's faults and evil treatment of me, I was to continue to keep my husband in my heart, to love him as God wanted me to but not become co-dependent. Now that is God's agape love! He loves His children in spite of our imperfections, He loves the whole world, but does not expect us to stay in sin and live in dangerous situations. I know of others who have fought for love, and lost their lives in the fight, but they are winners also. For Gods' love is greater than death. Follow the leading of the Lord at all times. He will tell you turn left or turn right, do this or do that. I said, "Yes Lord, I will love Ralph even while he's not being lovable".

I tried taking him with me to church, but he was so drunk that he began moving the seats around and being disruptive. Seeing this, an usher came over and asked us to sit in a special area. Again, attempting to get him to the Word, I took him and our children to a Billy Graham Crusade held in Rice Stadium. Big mistake, he stood up during the service cursing everyone. I ran out grabbing him and the children. I thought, if I can only get him to church Jesus would touch him and he would change. I knew the power in the blood of Jesus to save, heal, and deliver. No matter how hard the situation appeared there was nothing more powerful than the blood of Christ Jesus. The divine flow of love is reaching out to you now!

At this point I'd like to share four points critical to this juncture in my life:

1) The Lord was ordering my each and every step.

2) We, as children, need to listen and obey the voice of our Heavenly Father.

3) To live victorious in Christ and love as He loves, we must die to our flesh.

4) Attend a church where the pastors hear from God and preach life to the congregation from the Bible.

From these points God gives us a beautiful picture, instructing us to obey our earthly parents. How much more should we obey our heavenly Father that it may go well with us and that we will have a long and satisfied life? God has promised to order your steps as you are willing to hear His voice. The Bible says, *"My sheep hear my voice . . . The voice of a stranger they will not follow,"* (John 10:5 KJV). We are children of God, and He is a loving Father. He desires obedience in every area of our lives and we cannot obey if we don't hear His voice. We hear His voice clearly as we stay in the Word. It's so important to meditate and saturate daily in the Word of God. Joshua 1:8 says This book of the law shall not depart out of thy mouth; but thou shall meditate therein day and night, that thou may observe to do according to all that is written therein: for then thou shall make thy way prosperous, and then thou shall have good success. Setting aside a time of intimacy with the Lord is very important for our spiritual growth, because faith comes by hearing the Word of God. It causes the heart to be willing and obedient.

I remember as a child wanting to have my own way. Now each time I look back on the situation, my way of thinking brought me pain, sorrow and fear. We must die to self. Many Christians don't want to die to the flesh because at the time it seems painful. Dying involves saying, 'no' to our will and 'yes' to the will of God, for it is His thoughts and plans for our lives, the One who holds our future and knows every path we should take.

Galatians 5:16 (KJV) says, *"[This] I say then, Walk in the Spirit, and ye shall not fulfill the lust of the flesh." The lust of the eye, the pride of life, and the lust of the flesh will keep you from God's best. The flesh wants to rule, but there's no good thing in the flesh. Before we can receive God's plans our flesh must be crucified even if it hurts.*

It was very painful, at first, to love my husband who seemingly hated me. Until I found out the devil was the real enemy who hated me. Having to cook and clean for someone who despised me was challenging. Yes, it was agonizing having to check on him when the Spirit led me to do so. He spoke such cruel things to me, I did little things like seeing if he had eaten anything that day, he wasn't eating properly because of the drinking. Matthew 5:44 (KJV) says, *"But I say unto you, love your enemies, bless them that curse you, do good to them that hate you, and pray for them which despitefully use you, and persecute you; . . . .*" Don't think you're fighting flesh and blood. No! Your fight is with the powers of darkness. It's a good fight of faith, and we win using the Word of God, it's our spiritual weapon. When Jesus was in the wilderness tempted by the devil he overcame his tricks by speaking the Word of truth.

This was truly a journey an adventure of love. During these years of living out God's plan for loving my husband, God elevated me to a higher level of faith, because *"Faith worketh by love"* (Galatians 5:6 KJV). God is calling His body *to walk by faith and not by sight* (2 Corinthians 5:7).

Life is like a "maze," made up with many people of different races, origins, and creed. We each have different personalities, mindsets, educational backgrounds, goals, and dreams. Life has many twist and turns. Each day we make simple and vital choices pertaining to our lives whether to marry or not to marry, what career we want to enter or what school we would like to attend. What outfit to wear, what restaurant to eat at or what movie to watch. In any decision making we must first ask God for his wisdom and invite Jesus to make our life journey successful. "But seek ye first the kingdom of God, and His righteousness; and all these things will be added unto you"(Matthew 6:33 KJV). Pray, for He is all knowing and His wisdom has no end. We do not know what tomorrow holds, however God is calling us to come up higher into the plans that He predestined before the world began.

We are to be like Christ Jesus in the earth. He provided a great exchanged when the Divine became flesh so that we who are flesh could be partakers of his divine nature through his promises. Jesus stepped out of eternity into time so that we can go from time into eternity, life on earth is temporal but life with God is forever. There is always resurrection after crucifixion! You're not going under your going over. Keep yielding yourself to the Holy Spirit and don't go back to your old life, like a dog to his vomit (2 Peter 2:22). Today we can get caught up in the worldly dance of two steps where we take two steps up and two steps back which interns lead us back to the same place. Don't get stuck, be determined to press toward the mark of the high calling of God.

Keep moving forward. Cry out to God for your deliverance. A broken and contrite heart He will not despise. He will take you through the wilderness to your promised land, your destiny is a place of abundant life here on earth where all of God promises are "yes" and "amen" (so be it to me). God is faithful to His promises! Hallelujah!

Chapter Six
Help! What . . . ???

I've often wondered how such a tall, handsome man with such a brilliant mind, capable of repairing any vehicle, could be so blinded by demons. The mind of Christ is a healthy mind that's balanced; God first, family second, then work, and then friends. In trouble times we can look to the hills where our help comes from. Our help comes from God. Ralph was slowly dying and could not see himself nearing the edge (going crazy), even when he put the gasoline in his mouth. He blew the gasoline out of his mouth then lit it and the flames shot up in his face, he called it spitting fire. I thought that's what happened that day but Ralph said that the radiator blew up in his face. What I saw that day made the "maze" more difficult for me to understand. God said he always gives us a way of escape, just listen for His voice and obey. Ralph want his own way he soon became a derelict on "skid row," caring for neither himself nor anyone else. He roamed the streets with his hair wild and beard unkempt, having lost all desire to be in the company of his family. God tells us in 1Timothy 5:8, that if a man does not take care of his family he is worse than an infidel. Even pastors and ministers of every kind should make their family their first ministry, not their jobs.

Ralph's ambition now was to make just enough money to purchase alcohol. Liquor at this time was all he yearned for. He was living in our house which was beginning to look old and abandoned as there were no lights, gas, or running water. He spent every cent on drink.

Demons spoke through him in spooky, high-pitched voices, crying out, "Eiiiih, eiiiiih, we're taking him to hhheeeeellll"!

When visiting him one day as I often did in an effort to help him, I yelled back, "Not this husband you won't!" I confessed, "I am a covenant woman not moved by what I see or feel; only moved by the Word of God!" Even when I doubted God's promise that he would save my husband, I continued to confess God's rhema words of deliverance (I Corinthians 7:14).

Some friends at church as well as some co-workers advised me to leave Ralph. They said things like, "You can do better for yourself without him. You have a good job and you don't have to put up with this. God has better things for you Charlotte."

I know my friends meant well and they loved me, but I also knew what God's promises were to me. Whenever human reasoning stop you from believing the promises you get off of God's best plan for your life. When you feel there is no help in your own life and all the demons of hell seem to break loose against you, remember, *God will never leave you nor forsake you.* (Hebrews 13:5) *He is able to do, and will do superabundantly, far over and above all we dare ask or think according to the power working in us* (Ephesians 3:20). The Word works when we obey from a heart of love.

Not all my friends told me to leave, there were those who believed with me the whole way, never doubting; they were Thomas, Charlie, Allen, Saul, Linda, Chris,

Sue, Veronica, Gilda, Marcelle, Franklin, Ford and others. When I would share with them about the love of Jesus, they responded back with love, and I had the privilege of seeing them grow in the Lord. Some of them already knew the Lord and some came to know Him. Definitely what the enemy meant for evil, the Lord used for good. I became a passionate soul winner.

Suddenly in my most trying time, Jesus called me to teach His Word. I heard Him gently speak to my spirit, "I'm sending you to teach the Body of Christ."

Of course, I thought, "Jesus missed it. I can't speak, I'm too shy. What will I say? I'm too scared. I can't even talk to a person face to face."

My husband's mistreatment had taken its toll on my self-esteem. I had none, as life had so beaten me down;

but again, what the devil meant for evil and destruction in my life, God turned for His good! (Genesis 50:20). God lovingly chose me in the furnace of affliction, and I said, "Yes!" A 'yes' to God is a 'no' to the devil every time. It's an awesome thing to be chosen by God. He is calling you, too! He is calling everyone into new life in Christ Jesus, to be born again and to do a work for Him in building His Kingdom right here in the earth. We must choose to say 'yes' to God. I remember when my daddy said 'yes' to God; I was blessed to get to know my father well and see his life changed before he went to be with the Lord.

As I began to delve more deeply into the Word of God under the teaching of Pastor John Osteen at Lakewood Church, which was founded in an old feed store, I realized why God selected that location for its birthplace.

Pastor John fed the spirits of many individuals from all over the world in that place. For me particularly, it was a place where I could come and feed richly on God's holy Word. Though wounded, broken, and intensely hurt, I grew strong under Pastor Osteen's teachings. Lakewood became my lifeline. Proverbs 9:1 (KJV) says in part, *"Wisdom hath buildeth her house . . ."* I rarely missed a service. The wisdom of God through His Word was indeed building me up. I learned that man shall not live by bread along, but by every word that proceedeth out of the mouth of God.(Matthew 4:4 KJV).

His Word was now framing my choices, they were now based on the revelation I received from the Word. I was receiving the mind of Christ. The impossible was becoming possible with Christ. I was seeing a better picture of why I was created, to be salt and light. I shall forever thank God for Lakewood Church and Lisa Osteen Comes' class, 'Healing for Marriages' held on Tuesday nights. The classes taught us how to believe God for our mates' salvation and instructed us in prayer for unsaved loved ones. Class facilitators prayed with us and coached us to stand and not give up. Today the divorce rate is up in the church. We should strive to stay married until death do us apart. The good news is that when both are born again we will see our loved ones again. We would *surely reap a harvest of blessing if we faint not* (Galatians 6:9). Stay in the Word and don't give up, don't give in, and don't give out. The answer to your prayer is on the way.

The devil mockingly told me, "You'll be old and gray-haired before your husband will be saved."

I boldly told him, "If I wait to be one hundred years old before the promise manifests, I don't care." I remembered

Sarah how God preserved her in her old age for she was beautiful.

Remember Abraham and Sarah? (Genesis 17:15-21:7) They waited twenty-five years for the promised son, Isaac. God has a due season for His people. When the promise is made faith is required to receive it. The Word says in the book of Matthew 9:29 (KJV), *". . . . According to your faith be it unto you"*.

God's promises to me were being fulfilled despite the fact that I could not see it in the natural. I had to deal with both the shame of how my husband looked, and the shame of our troubled marriage. While I was in the "maze" at every turn the Lord in His mercy and grace kept me. He never once left me nor did He ever forsake me. In the midst of this shame the Lord told me, "No matter how Ralph looks I want you to love him unconditionally, even if he looks like a cockroach". The Lord Knew I hated roaches, the hatred came from living my childhood in poverty. One day the big roaches came after me like bees! They attacked me when I was sharing the good news of Jesus to Ralph. I was fighting them off but I never stopped the message I was sharing.

The Divine Artist knew this was an act of love that comes only from the Spirit of God. All this time the Lord was growing and maturing me in Him. He taught me to forgive. God showed me the beam in my own eyes and how to remove that while I was beholding the mote in my husband's eye (Matthew 7:3). As a rose I blossomed in the desert, this is a secret of the "maze." I had to be free of my selfish thoughts and the enemy's thoughts when he told me I was not going to make it. I took every thought captive to the obedience of the Word in order to receive Gods' thoughts on how to interact with my husband. I made a conscience effort to memorize scriptures that would lift my spirit but most of all confessing what Jesus said I was, what I can do, and what I could have. Confessing the same things that Jesus said in His Word are seeds that must be planted in our hearts and believed by faith.

The moment I received Christ (age 11), the bible says, I was born again and the fallen nature was taken away. However, I still had bad habits and thoughts that needed changing and also emotional trauma that needed healing. Believing God's Word will bring healing to your spirit, body and soul. Now I could make a choice to be lead by the Spirit from my inner man whom I would feed the Word of God. The veil of blindness was removed. I began a state of metamorphosis where the glory of God could be seen on me as I was growing in Christ image. The scriptures opened up a new world, a dimension in the Spirit where I felt the love of God. There was peace of mind and joy that only the Spirit can give in trouble times. It was during this time God was sending laborers across Ralph's path and working steadily behind the scenes, in the natural I could not see it, but in the Spirit He was arranging things, people, and places drawing him by the Spirit.

Our third child was born in the midst of this struggle, Kenyatta, our boy and a special gift at this time. *Know that God loves you. He has your back and is there for you even if you can't see your miracle yet. He is working it out while you are still trying to figure it out.* Baby Kenyatta has grown into a precious man of God in spite of our home being a virtual emotional roller coaster, with moments of fighting and making up, again and again. At the time, if anyone had asked, "Can anything good come out of the Jolivet household," I still would have answered, "Yes! God is faithful!" Kenyatta who is married to Patrice, has been called to preach the gospel and is a youth pastor at

Bailey Chapel Church of God in Christ in Waller, Texas. My dear late friend Rethena Lyons, was a preacher of the gospel prophesied to Kenyatta when he was five years old that he would preach the gospel and it has come to pass.

All I'd dreamed and more have come true. Today all our children are saved, sanctified and filled with the precious Holy Ghost. My first born, Elaine, is the mother of three beautiful, saved daughters. She does volunteer work with the Fifth Ward Pregnancy Center, and also through Harvest Time Church, she volunteers with Star of Hope Ministries, where she provide chapel service. Elaine also does sign language interpretation for the hearing impaired at her church. Ralph, Jr. who also attends Harvest Time Church with his wife Latresa, teaches a men's Bible study class. They have three wonderful sons. Hallelujah! Isaiah 54:13 says, *"All my children shall be blessed of the Lord and great shall be the peace of my children."* They have been a blessing in my life, so I encourage you to remember God is working behind the scenes perfecting all that concerns you.

I speak peace to your heart today. Peace on your job or in school; peace in your home; and peace in your marriage or where ever you are, Shalom. Freely, let the blood of Jesus cover every area of your life, for Jesus, the prince of peace, is coming to your house today. We will leave a legacy of the love of God to our children and down to a thousand generations. The verse God gave me as a promise for my husband's salvation was I Corinthians 7:14, *"The unbelieving husband is sanctified by the wife and the unbelieving wife is sanctified by the husband."* The second part of this verse was for my children's salvation, *"else your children was unclean but now are they holy."* God wants to help you before you get married, He said be not unequally yoke with unbelievers. Seek God first and if you have sinned and gotten off track pray and listen to God, He's better than your GPS.

Our beautiful grandchildren have been such a blessing to us. They have confessed Christ as savor. I want to mention them by name. We have three granddaughters Darneshia and Darnetta who are twins, and their younger sister is Dacora; and three grandsons Henning, Sven, and Earl. This is the decade of the testimony! I declare, every test we've walked through empowers us to be greater witnesses to the glory of God having overcome our enemy. *"For they overcame him by the blood of the Lamb and the word of their testimony, and they loved not their lives to the death."* (Revelation 12:11 KJV)

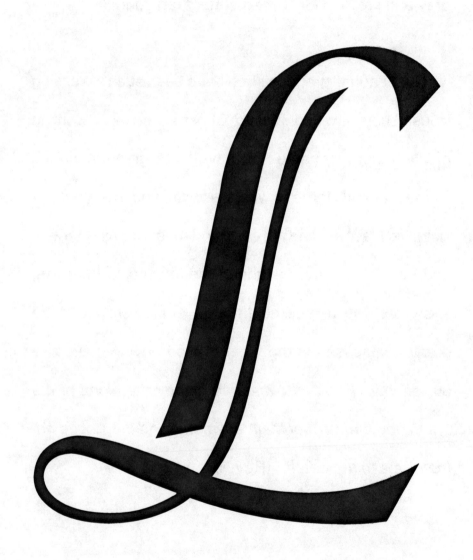

Chapter Seven

Breaking Point to Victory

The scene changes into pure darkness the darkest hour before dawn. Remember God created the whole world out of darkness; the Divine Artist is still working all things for your good, and what happens next was a turn around to victory. When you are twisted, tried, tested, and troubled on every hand and you stay faithful to the Word then you will come forth as pure gold. In the "maze" of life where everything can fail, God's love never fails and His Word always prevails. The breaking point came one night when Ralph was in a drunken stupor. He foolishly decided to turn on the electricity for a friend of his, whose home was without lights. Ralph climbed a telephone pole to reach the high voltage wires when he slipped, fell, and tore his leg nearly half off. His behavior reminded me of the mad man of Gadara. (what's driving you to your breaking point?) You can be overcome by any of life problems like the man in the book of Mark. Dwelling among the tombs represents the lies you dwell on in your mind (wrong thinking about your problems, yourself and God).

"And when he was come out of the ship, immediately there met him out of the tombs a man with an unclean spirit, who had his dwelling among the tombs; and no man could bind him, no, not with chains: because that he had been often bound with fetters and chains, and the chains had been plucked asunder by him, and the fetters

broken in pieces: neither could any man tame him. And always, night and day, he was in the mountains, and in the tombs, crying, and cutting himself with stones." (Mark 5:2-5 KJV)

An unclean spirit will cause you to isolate yourself becoming as the living dead. Demonic spirits never settle for a small part of an individual they have oppressed or possessed, they want full possession with the sole intent of stealing, killing, and ultimately destroying that person's life. *But thanks be to God who always causes us to triumph in Christ Jesus!* (2Corinthinians 2:14) The devil is no match for our God! Jesus defeated him at the cross, taking his weapons and totally stripping him of all power (Colossians 2:14-15). I stepped into a spiritual world of 3D (the real world) where there are no mediocre just different levels and different anointings. Where I decided to take the high road and receive all of God's good promises to me. A world that consist of extreme agape love, light, and "zoë" life, which causes us to believe, behave, and become a blessing, so that we can be a blessing.

Now, I was not just going to church I realized I was the church a supernatural, powerful, and righteous new creation that made up the body of Christ in the earth. We want extreme sports, lifestyles, and money. Why not extreme agape love? We should be known in three worlds; **Heaven**, where we are seated in heavenly places with Christ, **Earth** where we draw near to God by submitting to His will, and **Hell** where we resist the devil with The Word of God and he flees in terror. The Bible says we should live in the spirit, walk in the spirit and when we fall down we run to the Father to receive forgiveness and get his thoughts on the way we should act when we do this we are putting on the new man created in Christ Jesus. If we continue to grow in Christ we can breakthrough every strong hold of the enemy.

Mark 5:7-8, continues, *"And cried with a loud voice, and said, what have I to do with thee, Jesus thou Son of the most high God? I adjure thee by God, that thou torment me not. For he said unto him, Come out of the man, thou unclean spirit."* When Jesus says come out, he means *out!* Many times demons will tell a person that Jesus is the enemy, as demonstrated in this verse. But Jesus is never the tormentor; the devil and demons are the tormentors. Evil spirits want to convince their captive that God is the source of all their pain. The devil is a liar! Jesus said in John 8:44 (KJV), *". . . . When he speaketh a lie, he speaketh of his own; for he is a liar and the father of it."* But God is a good God! God can't lie. He is the deliverer.

He invites us to *"taste and see that the Lord is good"* (Psalms 34:8 KJV). That scripture was my sister, Nancy's, favorite. She received a miracle when a tumor was removed from her brain when she almost died. However, God healed her and added more years to her life. Many years later Nancy went home to be with the Lord whom she loved with all her heart. God is love and He wants to take sickness, sin, poverty, and death away from us. Stand my brother! Stand my sister! God is faithful. Even in what seems to be the darkest day of your life, God is faithful, and really the day your deliverance is speeding toward you. Trust and obey because there is no other way.

Ralph, after the fall had a deep tare to his leg. He took a needle and thread to sew the wound up himself! This was horrifying to us, the whole scene was crazy, and the worse part was that he showed no evidence of pain or discomfort while trying to repair the wound. There was such emptiness in him; he seemed void of natural responses. The effects of sin will leave you empty and take you further down than you ever want to go; yet, in this tragic moment, God was still working. It was distressing and beyond belief to watch as Ralph put the needle through his oozing flesh; there was blood everywhere. One of his friends heard me screaming, I was crying, praying, and begging Ralph to allow me to take him to a hospital, but he wouldn't go. His friend somehow managed to convince him to go. Praise God! Cry out to Jesus and He will answer in ways you often least expects. He will fill your times of feeling helpless, fearful, and chaotic, with His love, joy, and peace.

In the hospital Ralph could not drink. Bless God! His mind began to sober during the month and a half stay, and I realized that he was not blinded by the spirit of alcohol anymore (2Corinthians 4:4) The devil blinds the mind and when the light of the gospel shines through to the lost then it sets them free. It was then that God released him from his chains of captivity. The devil had to let my husband go!

Whenever we came up to visit him, we were ministering the love of Jesus to him (Galatians 4:5) Christ came to redeem those under law, that we might receive the full rights of sons. The law could not save us. The law only showed us how sinful we are and that we need a Saviour. Our fallen nature is taken away in Christ we become a new creature old things are passed away and all things become new (2Corinthians5:17). The art of love works, Ralph confessed that he had seen something different in me, the peace, love of God, and the consistency of my faith was also drawing him to

God. What the law could not do Love did. Rules without relationship create rebellion. We love because He first loved us.

One day on a routine visit to the hospital I asked, "Ralph, do you now want to accept Jesus into your heart as your personal Saviour?" "Yes", he immediately answered. Praise God for His awesome goodness and indescribable love. At that moment I felt as if the heavens opened and we were all transported into a place of security in Him, the Glory! God's manifested presence is that supernatural place, in which no evil can ever win in our lives again; a place where nothing but the intimacy and presence of Christ matters. We were dancing with the angels among the stars; there were shouts of joy both in the room and in the heavenly as we gave God worship and praise for His amazing grace.

The gospel (the Good News) always demands a response, 'yes' or 'no', but a choice has to be made by you. A conscious decision has to be made because there is no neutral grounds. This decision is for the living and not the dead. Jesus just needs one righteous seed, meaning someone who is born again and has faith enough to believe God for their generation, to pass the blessing to a thousand generations to come. Matthew 11:12 (KJV) reads," . . . *the kingdom of heaven suffers violence, and the violent take it by force."* Faith that works by love is a force, it is an act of obedience, and obedience is a spiritual weapon.

"I call heaven and earth to record this day against you, that I have set before you life and death, blessing and cursing: therefore choose life, that both thou and thy seed may live" (Deuteronomy 30:19 KJV). God's entire plan is

an act of love towards us. Even in the garden where He planted the two trees, only one tree He didn't allow Adam and Eve to eat of. It was the tree of knowledge of good and evil. It was not an apple tree, people have always focused on the fruit, let us deal with the root cause. If God is always thinking of our good, which he is according to (Jeremiah 29:11); they could have chosen to eat of the tree of life and would live forever in fellowship with God. Living in fellowship with God would have been God's perfect plan. Living in His will, will always bring us into a good destiny. The devil, which is called the tempter, caused them to disobey and they chose to listen to the enemy's voice and eat from the tree of knowledge of good and evil. He wanted them to lose out on God's original plan, and they would take on his evil nature, and never know the goodness of our God. Oh, the wisdom of God who would create a win-win situation.

I believe eating of the tree brought sin into the world and it also produced the conscience. The enemy wanted us to be losers like him but God knows that we are winners! The plan of God was to trump the enemy's scheme and when Adam part-took of the fruit, it imparted the knowledge of good back into the human race.

The consequence of the original sin in the garden caused us to make choices to do good or evil. You've heard the saying let your conscience be your guide, it will tell you if something is evil then turn around and show you something good about it. Your conscience will accuse, and excuse you. (Romans 2:15) Only when we choose Christ, we choose life, and we are able to be lead by the Spirit (God's GPS) into the abundant life. Those that are led by the spirit of God are the sons of God (Romans 8:14). The conscience is clean only through renewing it with the Word once we're born again. Hypothetically, if we made all the right choices all the time in this sin cursed world by using our conscience it could never impart God's righteousness in our fallen nature. All of our righteousness is as filthy rags (Isaiah 64:6). When we believe in Jesus, righteousness is imputed in us and we are blessed (James 2:23) Jesus took our sins on the cross and gave us His righteousness.

This is good news, to every sinner; you can turn to Christ and receive His righteousness. (Jeremiah 29:11 . . . I know the thoughts I have towards you, saith the Lord, thoughts of peace, and not of evil, to give you an expected end). All of God's thoughts are good towards us and He has already worked them out when He said it is finished. Sin blinds us from knowing the goodness of God, but when we see His goodness it leads us to repentance. He changed my life and now I desire to do His will and help bring restoration to others. It doesn't matter what kind of home you're born in, rather functional or dysfunctional, you can be born again. Life is to complex you can't make it on your own; it's not by your might nor by your power but by the Spirit of God that we survive. The kingdom of God came to our house and now it's coming to you *"I have told you these things, so that in me you may have peace. In this world you will have trouble. But take heart! I have overcome the world."*—John 16:33.

THE CHOICE IS YOURS!

The strongman is an evil spirit that's determined to bind you and keep you from your divine destiny. This evil spirit comes through the doors of bitterness, unforgiveness, wrong thinking, even trauma, and every sin. The strongman shows up in our sinful action, our bad habits and attitudes. To get rid of this spirit it has to first be bound. Matthew 12:25-30 (KJV) states: ". . . , every kingdom divided against itself is brought to desolation: and every city or house divided against itself shall not stand: and if Satan cast our Satan, he is divided against himself, how shall then his kingdom stand? And if I by Beelzebub cast out devils, by whom do your children cast them out? Therefore they shall be your judges. But if I cast out devils by the Spirit of God, then the kingdom of God is come unto you. Or else how can one enter into a strongman's house, and spoil his goods, except he first bind the strongman? And then he will spoil his house. He that is not with me is against me; and he hath gathereth not with me scattereth abroad." We should always take our spiritual authority.

You can close the door by saying yes to Jesus. Now that you can feel and see the goodness of God and how much he loves you. I know your heart is prepared to say yes to his will in every situation. So, will you say 'yes' to Jesus? How beautiful and rich is His grace that God would use me to lead my husband to Him; Ralph, the very man who tormented me through the years with cursing, fighting, strife, and neglect had now become a born again Christian. What an awesome God we serve! How I thanked Jesus Christ as I led Ralph in the sinner's prayer. He was saved and filled with the Holy Ghost. Thank You, Jesus! If you ask Jesus to come into your heart, He will come in. He will save you and change your life. *"For whosoever shall call upon the name of the Lord shall be saved"* (Romans 10:13 KJV).

This is truly one of the greatest love stories ever told. God utilized me as a conduit for another's life which is the great commission to go into all the world and preach the gospel to every creature, and he that beliveth in Jesus shall be saved,(Mark 16:15-18). Also the greatest commandment, is to love God with all you heart with all your soul and all your mind, and to love others (Matthew 22:37-39). God shared His agape love with me and allowed me to love my husband in the same manner.

While I pray no one will ever go through the pain and misery I experienced in my marriage, I know nothing is too hard for the Lord. God will turn your situation around. Romans 8:28 says, *"And we know that in all things God works for the good of those who love him."* This familiar passage does not stop there it continue to say, *"for those who love Him and are called according to His purpose."* Our God is a God of purpose and He never fails. He will bring you through the battle to victory. The "maze" has become my friend because now, I have learned to die daily and our hearts are knitted as one with the Lord. Each time we yield to the spirit our flesh dies therefore we can say **NO** to sin by the power of the Spirit. Greater is He that is in you than he that is in the world. Only when we lose our life we will find it. Life is the most cherished gift from God, it is a present that should be lived each moment to His glory.

The Divine Artist, who is our heavenly father, has created us for His greater glory and designed a perfect plan for your good it's the blessed and best life for us. Today my husband and I are both winners. God has made us both champions and overcomers in this life. Don't let life break you down mentally, physically, or spiritually. You can break out into victory. This wonderful miracle came about all because Jesus died on the cross at Calvary for sinners. Thank **You**, Jesus!

He signed this work of art . . . . touched by the Master's hand.

God cares for you and He wants to use you, so surrender yourself totally to Him. Make a conscience decision that you will turn from sin and that you will serve the true and living God with passion. Receive all God has for you, he is faithful. My whole family is now born-again and serving the Lord. Ralph is free from alcohol; the taste has been removed from his taste buds and he has no desire for it. Glory to God! We have found our place with the Lord and share a beautiful home of peace where our Lord Jesus, the Prince of Peace, abides. What I once thought was ideal, living like playing in a 'doll's house', was nothing but fantasy. Why live in fantasy and lies when you can have reality and truth. Praise God! I now know the truth that only in Jesus can you live a genuinely good, prosperous, healthy, and happy life (the "maze"). We should not let the world mold us into its standards, for we are in the world but not of the world (Romans 12:2). Together, we've survived and come through some of life's darkest storms, If led by the Spirit maybe at another time I will share more of these storms. They have all been life lessons to victory. I have learned to remain in the sweet spot of God's will even when the storms of life rage. Chastisement pruning and deliverance are a part of God's never ending love.

Ralph's metamorphosis was a journey where God completely restored his mind, his body, and his spirit and he received double blessings for his trouble. My shining knight has become a shining light for Jesus. When anyone shares Ralph's testimony God's light shines through that man might see the glory of God and there in the glory we are changed, many have received Christ. It's because of God's awesome, unconditional, enduring love for His children, we have survived by the power of the greatest love story ever told, for this is His story. For God so loved the world that He gave His only begotten son that if we believe we will not parish but have everlasting life. Mankind has sin and fallen short of the glory of God. Jesus died while we were yet sinners so we can step back into His glory where everything changes and becomes new. Our surviving has now turned into thriving. Glory! Glory! Glory! Now that's heavy—Heavy! Heavy! Heavy! God has done so many great things for me, I just can't tell it all. Thank God for the many seasons in our lives. Ralph no longer wants to swim in the bayou with the alligators; he only watches them on the nature channel. Thank God for that.

My quest of seeking what this life is all about, even when I know the economy is down and we have just finished the Iraq war, and that the extreme weather is affecting everyone and Obama is now the President. Life still have many surprising twist and turns, that is why we need the light of God's word where we find His love and we share it with the world. Only what you do for Christ will last in this world. At any age you can find true agape love. This love can be found in the redeeming work of Christ. God has given me beauty for ashes and the garment of praise, for the spirit of heaviness. Therefore at sixty-two having been married forty six years to Ralph, the most important things in our life are **family** and **friends** who live by **faith** in the Son of God who loved us and gave His life. We are the ones who chose the supernatural 3D life by living God's extreme Agape. Where even your **foe** (enemy) will be at peace with you and it will draw them to trust and believe in God. We are blessed to be a blessing. We also realize that we need each other and it is God's voice (GPS) that we all must follow to have an abundant life. We live from the new created spirit in Christ Jesus it's called the new creation and not from our fallen nature (the old man). Our faith works by love that causes us to reach out to a hurting world in order to bring in the end time harvest. This is winning in life and I give God all the glory, because of all He's done for me. It makes falling in love with Jesus the greatest thing that ever happened to me. I Am Love's Survivor!

Acknowledgement

I would like to thank God for using Lisa Osteen Comes, Dodie Osteen, the late Pastor John Osteen and the entire Lakewood Church family for their support, spiritual teachings, and prayers of faith and love. I too, thank my mom, our families and friends for praying with and for us. I am also very grateful to my bible study group at the U. S. Postal Service, and all who obeyed Jesus in laboring and blessing our lives.

I would also like to thank our present pastor, Joel Osteen, for leading us into a new place of thriving. I am able to minister to the hurting, and as I do so, I feel that I am passing on the love I have received. Love is not love until you give it away. While helping others to receive the Word of God they too are being empowered and raised to a new level of hope, giving God the glory He so richly deserves.

Prayer of Salvation

Jesus, I invite You to come into my heart and forgive me for my sins. I believe that You died on the cross and rose again for me, therefore I ask You to live in me, to save me, deliver me, and be my Lord and Saviour. I thank You that I am now a new creature in Christ, and from this day forward I am the address of God where Jesus lives. In Jesus' name I pray. Amen.

In the book I prophesied that this is the decade of the testimonies. So begin writing your testimony today. Joyce Meyer in 2002 sent me an encouraging letter about my testimony and Lisa Comes just released her awesome testimony "You are made for more".

The day Debra Duncan asked me to be on her TV show, the Lord started changing the ashes of my life into beauty. He will do the same for you.

Love's Survivor

Love's Survivor

Charlotte Jolivet

Love's Survivor

Charlotte Jolivet

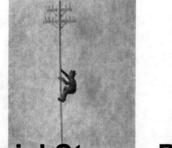

My Memorial Stones Pictures

Joshua 4: 6-7

6. That this may be a sign among you, that when your children ask their fathers in time to come, saying, What mean ye by these stones?

7. Then ye shall answer them, That the waters of Jordan were cut off before the ark of the covenant of the LORD; when it passed over Jordan, the waters of Jordan were cut off: and these stones shall be for a memorial unto the children of Israel for ever.

Taken from www.BibleGateway.com

Mrs Louis our Neighbor, Mamie, Queenie, Nancy, Charlotte and Elizabeth

Jerome and Queenie

Nancy

Ralph and Charlotte

Betty, Elizabeth, Charlotte, Mamie

A love that lasted

Our first child Elaine at the park.

1966
Ralph had the ability to repair
a car in side and out

Going off the edge

Some of the thing
that was thrown outside

Some of the thing
that was thrown outside

It look like he was spiting fire

Church Day

The Maze of Life

The beginning of the shop

Jackie, Paula, Carla, Valerie Ann and my nephews were not present, when this picture was taken.

My sisters and our daughter's with my daughter-in-law

Ralph's six sisters

Ralph and his nine brothers

Lisa healing for marriage

Ralph and I marriage restored

At a church wedding

Friends and family at Lakewood

CLASS OF 1968
Me, mom and dad, and Mamie

CLASS OF 2011
Darneshia, Grandma, Darnetta, and Elaine

Mom and her children at Gilbert Blake's funeral, my stepfather

A snap shot at the repast. Mom went to be with Jesus, in 2011

Our children and grandchildren, with daughter-in-law LaTresa

I have met people I never thought I would meet.
Gone places I never thought I would go.
I am headed for Israel, the place where my Jesus was born.
A dream trip come true.

Ralph a life changed by Love now an ordain Chaplain

CPSIA information can be obtained at www.ICGtesting.com
Printed in the USA
LVOW11s0819181113

361662LV00003B/149/P